"Some books are to be tasted, others to be swallowed and some few to be chewed and digested; that is, some books are to be read only in parts; others to be read but not curiously; and some few to be read wholly and with diligence and attention…"

Francis Bacon (1561 – 1626)

Henry G Dobson (2004)

Acknowledgements

The great majority of buildings featured in my book require no special acknowledgement.

I am especially grateful to owners of properties which do not fall into this category for the opportunity to take my photographs and hope that their being prominently presented and described as part of Newcastle's many attractions is reward enough.

I am also grateful for the continuing support of my wife, Susan, and for the invaluable technical assistance of both Ron Hodgson and Pat Hughes: thank you all.

Published by H G Dobson

Printed and bound by Martins the Printers Ltd,
Sea View Works, Spittal, Berwick upon Tweed

Introduction

There is presently an abundance of excellent books, of a largely photographic nature, available to aficionados of local interest and dealing with the social, cultural, industrial and architectural history of Newcastle upon Tyne; books which admirably illustrate the City's distinguished and fascinating past. Many of these books have two things in common: the photographs are almost exclusively black and white and, secondly, they almost invariably portray the City's past – Newcastle at the end of the 19th century; at the beginning of the 20th century; between the wars; in the '50s and '60s, and so on. That they are a wonderful and important social record of the City's metamorphosis and striking development is beyond question. Moreover, they are of immense interest particularly to people born before or during the Second World War, who can identify many of the subjects portrayed and who may sigh, nostalgically, at the sights they remember from their childhood with undisguised pleasure and affection – the bustling shipyards and the magnificent vessels built all along the Tyne; the tram cars and trolley buses, once a familiar and popular feature of the City's streets; street scenes, busy markets and shops, theatres, pubs and picture houses; footballers with baggy shorts and their flat capped supporters; contemporary fashion styles and engaging characters once as easily recognisable as many of the grimy buildings that punctuate the skyline.

To anyone under the age of five and twenty, however, some of these old photographs have as much relevance as pictures of medieval or Elizabethan Newcastle for it would surely be unreasonable to expect today's young people to truly relate to what they have never seen. They may, out of politeness, demonstrate a passing interest but, through no fault of their own, the natural empathy, the emotional attachment, is bound to be missing.

The Newcastle of the present is a vibrant, confident, modernising city increasingly at ease with the twenty first century and proudly aware of its growing importance and pre-eminence in the region. Thankfully, it has somehow succeeded – despite the 'barbarians hammering at the gates' – to hang on to much of its glorious heritage.

There are still many people who angrily mourn what they consider the mindless destruction inflicted on the City in the 1960s and '70s when those with the power to do so were resolute in their determination to create a fanciful "Brasilia of the North". Instead, so it is asserted, these so-called 'visionaries' wantonly destroyed far too much of what should, arguably, have been preserved and created, in lieu, soulless monuments to their mismanagement and forceful ambition.

But, rightly or wrongly, what was done is done and cannot be undone. Fortunately, however, despite the sometimes ill-conceived 'improvements' of that vexed period much remains in this "City of Palaces" to delight, surprise and excite the inquisitive observer – not just the 'crown jewels' of Grey Street and Grainger Street but the many less obvious 'gems' scattered in profusion around the town.

I have already referred to the plethora of absorbing publications devoted to Newcastle's past, enough to satisfy the voracious appetites of even the most fastidious student of 'old Newcastle'. I salute those who have diligently researched, assembled and published this fascinating material – yet nowhere have I found a collection of contemporary photographs dedicated to the Newcastle of the present... of the year 2004.

"City Sights" is no more than a humble effort seeking to redress this imbalance. My choice of subjects, as one might expect, is entirely arbitrary and so, inevitably I suppose, will immediately raise the question – "Why has he not included...?" The simple answer is – space!

Had I included every subject worthy of merit the book would have been encyclopedic in volume and commercially impossible. Even to accommodate my choice of subjects it has proved necessary to publish the book in two volumes (- the second of which should be available by the end of 2005).

"City Sights" lays no claim to be a definitive photographic record of contemporaneous Newcastle: for the reasons given it could not aspire to be so.

It is probably true to say that most of Newcastle's many visitors rarely stray far from the attractions of Northumberland Street and it's enticing emporia – apart, that is, from the 50,000 or so who regularly and in all weathers wind their way to the imposing concrete temple that is St James' Park football stadium, to watch "the Magpies" engage a rival from the Premier League or an opponent in one of the several domestic and European cup competitions.

But it would surely be absurd to suggest that while perhaps a majority of visitors are indeed content to spend their hours in one or other of these venues there are not others (- and not a few from overseas) far more interested in exploring and digesting – either on foot or on an open-topped touring bus – the City's history and traditions, its culture and its splendid architectural spectacles.

To these dear souls I dedicate my book, in the hope that what it reveals will inspire these same intrepid investigators to consciously stray from the hectic and hypnotic commercial thoroughfares of Northumberland Street and the incomparable Grainger Town and discover for themselves some of the many gems, obliquely referred to earlier, that the City of Newcastle is eager to reveal to its more discerning and perceptive visitor.

If "City Sights" is successful in this simple objective then it will have achieved its purpose and satisfied the author.

Index

All Saints Church	Pilgrim Street
Assembly Rooms	Fenkle Street
(The) Bank of England (Building)	Grey Street
Bewick's Workshop (site of)	Amen Corner
Black Gate	Castle Garth
Brunswick Methodist Chapel	Brunswick Place
Carliol House	Northumberland St. & Market St. East
Cathedral Buildings	Dean Street
Cathedral of St Nicholas	St Nicholas Street
Central Exchange	Grey Street
Church of St Ann	City Road
Church of St Thomas	Barras Bridge
Clavering House	Clavering Place
(The) Collingwood Memorial	The Side
County Court House	Westgate Road
(Joseph) Cowen Memorial	Westgate Road
Dame Allen's School	Northumberland Road and College Street
Eldon Square	Blackett Street
(Alderman) Fenwick's House	Pilgrim Street
Forth House	Thomas Bewick Square
(The) Gateshead Millennium Bridge	Quayside
Grainger Market	Grainger Street
Grainger Street	
(The) Guildhall	Sandhill
Higham Place	
Holy Jesus Hospital	City Road
International Centre for Life	Times Square
Joint Stock Bank	Mosley Street
Keelmen's Hospital	City Road
Laing Art Gallery	New Bridge Street
Leazes Terrace	
Lloyd's Bank	Grey Street
Memorials in the grounds of St Thomas'	Barras Bridge
Nelson Street	
Northumberland Baths (etc)	Northumberland Road

Northumberland Street (statues)	
Nun Street	
Police Headquarters	Market Street East
Royal Arcade	Pilgrim Street
Royal Victoria Infirmary	Queen Victoria Road
Sandhill	
St Mary's Place	
Stephenson Memorial	Westgate Road
Sutherland Building	Northumberland Road and College Street
Theatre Royal	Grey Street
(The) Tyne Bridge	
Wall Knoll (Sallyport Tower)	Tower Street
Westgate Road	

Described as "perhaps the best looking church in town" All Saints Church is built on the site of an older church - All Hallows – which, in turn, is said to have 'risen from the ruins' of a Roman Parthenon Temple. Throughout the 18th century the fabric of the medieval Church of All Hallows had deteriorated progressively and alarmingly. The east wall collapsed in 1699; a vestry window fell out in 1753 and the pillars of the south aisle collapsed in 1785. Yet throughout these difficulties it was still possible to hold regular church services!

In 1785 the churchwardens invited the Newcastle architect, William Newton, to give a detailed report of the church's sorry plight. His report, when it was finally delivered, confirmed their worst fears and made depressing reading – subsiding foundations leading to cracks in the masonry, leaning walls and pillars: problems which could not easily or cheaply be resolved.

Newton's proposals amounted to partial demolition and partial repair – at an estimated cost of £1,683.

There was understandably some debate and disagreement among the churchwardens over Newton's plan. A 'second opinion' was called for: David Stephenson and Ralph Dodds were consulted and their conclusion was that, all things considered, it would probably cost less, in the long run, to build a new church than to meet the growing expense of repairing the existing one. Newton stuck adamantly to his point of view but, after some deliberation and at a meeting of parishioners held on the 18th of April (1786) it was decided to build a new church. Advertisements were placed in local papers seeking plans for the new church and though designs were submitted (though, interestingly, none was forthcoming from Newton!) it was David Stephenson's which was accepted – partly, it was said, on the grounds of cost.

At twenty-nine years of age he was a relatively inexperienced architect, though he had been well trained in architecture at the Royal Academy Schools, in London. Moreover, and perhaps tellingly, Newton enjoyed the patronage of Newcastle's Mayor, Sir Matthew White Ridley. Sir Matthew was Chairman of the Vestry Committee whose brief was to select the winning design for the new church and as the Mayor's protégé it could be argued that Stephenson enjoyed a clear advantage. The final cost of the church was c.£27,000 but, as one writer in congratulatory terms expressed it, "the result was undoubtedly one of the best English churches of the period".

All Saints Church

The steeple (which was added in 1795) consists of a square tower, from which rises a series of stages, terminating in a light and elegant spire. All Saints, the mother church of St Ann's, on City Road, was built between 1786-96 to designs by David Stephenson, the first Newcastle man to study architecture in London.

The church has been described as 'an extraordinarily satisfying building, sophisticated in its oval plan and classical elevations and with a superb tower and spire which, surprisingly, were only an afterthought'.

Note the pedimented, detached portico standing on four Greek Doric columns at the front of the tower.

The stone ball on the top of the steeple is thirty inches in circumference and when it was placed in position one Private John Burdikin, of the Cheshire Militia (and afterwards a barber in Gateshead) climbed the scaffolding and stood on his head, his feet in the air, upon the stone ball – 194 feet above the ground!

During some repairs to the steeple in 1816, Burdikin's son repeated his father's outrageous and extremely dangerous feat.

Built between 1786-1796 All Saints is a rare British example of an elliptical church in the Renaissance style.

Consecrated in 1789 it was deconsecrated in 1961, by which time the church was considered too far from the mainstream of city life – in short, it had outlived its usefulness.

Since that date it has been given a new lease of life having been bought by the City Council, in 1970, who have since renovated it and given it to an organisation called Town Teacher Ltd.

Planned by William Newton and built between 1774-6, in what were then the grounds of St John's Church, a special Act of Parliament was needed before the work could begin, as the Vicar of St John's held the lease.

Described by David Lovey as "a splendid, neo-classical, symmetrical building with Greek Columns, handsome but simple windows and tasteful lower wings". The building cost £6,700.

The Assembly Rooms became a focal point for public meetings, debates; grand, colourful balls as well as select, private parties.

Fashionable cities like York and Bath already had Assembly Rooms – York's (of 1732) are described as "somewhat less refined and elegant": Bath's (of 1771) as "comparable in scale and quality", but, whereas Bath's had to be restored, having been severely damaged during World War II, Newcastle's are substantially original and were the first to be built in any industrial city anywhere in England.

The building comprises a brick body with polished stone facade: the canopy or portico over the main entrance is an unfortunate 20th century addition. Newton's design, both inside and out, is supremely elegant: all its features reflects its neo-classical taste – "the subtly articulated flatness of the facade; the windows of its low wings, set in semi-circular arches and the paired columns at either end of the central block".

The capitals of the six, Ionic columns are of special interest, being particularly un-Palladian in type: they derive from the Ionic order of the Erechtheion, on the Acropolis.

The interior, especially of the ballroom, with its seven, magnificent chandeliers (one of which is said to have cost six hundred guineas), and the fine plaster work, is "a superb example of provincial, decorative design, completely in the Adam manner".

The pilasters, for example, "have lost all pretence of a functional role and are merely vehicles for decoration".

"The Tyneside Classical Tradition", describes it as "… certainly the finest, neo-domestic interior in the region."

There were also card rooms, a library, newsroom, a coffee room and a huge, supper room.

The pediment is supported by the giant Ionic columns, paired at either end of the central block.

The windows of the wings, set in their semi-circular arches reflect the building's neo-classical taste.

The front is marred by an incongruous and rather tasteless twentieth century canopy.

The Bank of England (Building)   (33-41 Grey Street)

The centrepiece of the magnificent west side of Grey Street: it was
built by Richard Grainger c.1835 for the Bank of England and the
Northumberland and Durham District Banking Co, 'in the manner
of a grand palazzo', and is probably the design of John Wardle.

Of ten bays: the heavily moulded windows on the first floor are all pedimented and are separated by nine, twenty-five feet tall, fluted Corinthian columns – a Corinthian pilaster at either end.

The fourth floor attic is completely hidden by a fine balustrade: the rusticated ground floor is now an 'eatery' with the name Barluga.

The location of the workshop is now occupied by Milburn House
and a bust of the master engraver is set into an alcove in the wall of
this building, in Amen Corner or St Nicholas' Churchyard as it was
in Bewick's time. The building was originally owned by Joseph
Barber, a bookseller, who had let one part to Ralph Beilby for use
as a workshop and Barber used the adjoining smaller part for his
own business. But after Bewick went into partnership with his old
master they took larger and better premises in the south-east corner
of the churchyard: this move took place in 1795.

Thomas Bewick was born at Cherryburn House, on Mickley Bank,
in what was then the parish of Ovingham, in August 1753 and was
the eldest in a family of eight children. He died in 1828 and is
buried in St Mary's, Ovingham.

The Black Gate is said to get its name from one Patrick Black, a local 17th century magnate, and was formerly the main entrance to the Castle. It is believed to have been built in 1247, by Henry III, at a cost of £513-15-11.

It is a barbican gate set well away from the main gate behind it. It is roughly oval in shape, that is a gateway between two semi-circular guardrooms. The gateway is in three parts: an outer, with a portcullis; a middle with a gate and then a vaulted inner part. In front was a drawbridge. On the top of the two lower floors a brick house with mullioned and transomed windows was erected after 1618.

The lower part of the building, with its arched passage and vaulted guard-chambers, is mostly original work.

The upper part, with its square, mullioned windows, was largely rebuilt by Alexander Stevenson, who leased the building from James I. The fourth floor, with its steep tiled roof, is a modern addition.

Photographed by kind permission of the Society of Antiquaries.

In 1855 much of the property around the Black Gate was cleared
away to make a road to the High Level Bridge. The Black Gate was
threatened with demolition but this raised such a public outcry that
the threat was withdrawn. After much campaigning the building
was skilfully restored by R J Johnson and it presently houses the
library of the Society of Antiquaries of Newcastle, a body founded
in 1813. Their splendid collection of archaeological artefacts, from
pre-history and the Roman and Anglo-Saxon periods, has largely
been transferred to the Museum of Antiquities, in Newcastle
University.

The Black Gate is described as 'one of the most picturesque
combinations of medieval architecture existing in any English city'.

Brunswick Methodist Church (Brunswick Place)

Eneas Mackenzie (1827) wrote that it was built after the plan of Waltham Street Chapel, in Hull, and was constructed by the architect W Sherwood, in 1820-21.

It is a five-bay, two-storey building of brick with ashlar dressings: wide steps lead up to a double door inside a heavy Tuscan porch with prominent cornice.

Carliol House (now 'Fat Sam's')
(Northumberland Street and Market Street)

Constructed between 1924-8 for the North East Electric Company, the building takes its name from the Carliol family, wealthy 13th century merchants who lived in the town.

A most impressive building (described in 1950 as "the finest modern building in the city"), of Portland-clad-stone and "of classic proportions with the barest of classical decorative motifs".

The rounded, three-bay corner leading into Northumberland Street, with its ascending series of glass-marked storeys, rises to a low, lead dome way above the central entrance. No fewer than twenty-eight bays sweep around the corner into Market Street East without so much as a single pavilion.

Certainly the most colourful and picturesque buildings on Dean
Street and dating from 1901.

The ground floor (left to right) consists of a music shop, 'Sounds Live', separated by the Buildings' entrance from the 'Marco Polo' restaurant – both of which have a lovely pair of Jacobean columns lending support to the interesting window layout above.

The Cathedral Church of St Nicholas   (Newcastle upon Tyne)

The original Church of St Nicholas was founded by St Osmond, Bishop of Salisbury, in the time of William the Conqueror. Henry I granted it to the canons of St Mary's, Carlisle: this building was burnt down in 1216. The present church (it became a Cathedral in 1882) dates back to the middle of the 14th century. From 1784-87 the church was the subject of restoration "which left it bare of nearly all its monuments and brasses".

In 1867 the steeple was entirely repaired and in 1873 the restoration of the body of the church began.

The church was reopened on the 31st of May, 1877.

"The steeple of this church is very lofty and its top, which is built in the form of an imperial crown, is a work of admirable lightness and elegance. Its arches and knotted pinnacles in every direction are thrown into lines of great delicacy; and at four points of view the light through its centre assumes the form of a well-proportioned wheat-sheaf."

This part is said to have been added at the time of Henry VI.

The Exchange is a rich and beautiful semi-circular building imbedded in a triangle of noble houses, whose fronts are in Grey Street, Grainger Street and Market Street. Seven entrances lead from these streets to the Exchange. It is a semi-circle about one hundred and fifty feet long by one hundred feet in width, wholly lighted from above, as the building is encased in a triangle of houses. The roof is supported by fourteen Ionic columns, twelve of which form a semi-circle and within the columned area of this semi-circle is the News room – on the outskirts of the semi-circle are the corridors, entrances and staircases leading to the Coffee room and other apartments. Above the entablature, round the top of the semi-circle, spring a series of curved ribs, one over each column and these ribs form the skeleton for a magnificent glass dome, through which descends ample light into the area of the room. In an upper part of the building are Apartments for the School of Design. The triangle of houses within which the Exchange is thus singularly placed are of uniform design – the front presented towards the three streets are each an adaptation of the design of the Corinthian Temple of Vesta, at Rivoli – and the three points of the triangle are each finished by a dome springing from a nearly circular range of Corinthian columns.

(The Northumberland Directory of 1854.)

The Central Exchange was built between 1836-38, with the Central Exchange Hotel being added in 1862.

The triangular Exchange, with its domed roof, contained apartments, a coffee room and a news room.

It had many connections with the art world and housed the Victorian School of Art and the Northumberland Institute for Fine Arts. There was also an art gallery situated here in the 1870s. In the early '90s it was home to the Vaudeville Theatre, which held concerts and pantomimes.

Unfortunately, the original dome structure was gutted by fire in the early 1900s and was rebuilt as the picturesque Central Arcade, in 1905.

The Central Exchange triangle is a particularly interesting construction. Each of its sides is straight and symmetrical; its corners are rounded and domed and decorated with Greek honeysuckle motifs around the parapets and acanthus leaf finials.

Domed corner towers like these are a feature of Nash's London streets of the 1820s but their ultimate origin is French rather than English.

The corner of Market Street and Grainger Street.

It extends over an area of 11,835 square feet and is roofed by a magnificent glass dome from which light streams into the hall through 10,000 squares of glass.

David Lovie tells us that Grainger built this triangular building to house a new corn-market but the Corporation declined his offer. So, on the 19th of June, 1839, Grainger opened the Exchange as a 'subscription news-room'. Within three years there were nearly 1,600 members each paying a guinea per annum. There were surrounding coffee rooms and apartments with views overlooking the fashionable streets. The news-room later became an art gallery, concert hall and (in 1897) the Vaudeville Theatre.

In 1905 the entire building was reconstructed and the present shop-lined Central Arcade was cut through from Grey Street to Market Street with a link to Grainger Street.

There has been a church on this site since medieval times.

The present church, designed by William Newton, and built for the Newcastle Corporation (1764-8) as a chapel-of-ease for David Stephenson's All Saints' Church, at the bottom of Pilgrim Street, was consecrated in 1768.

The church was built largely using stone from the old city wall and its churchyard contains the graves of many who died in the last great cholera epidemic to hit the city.

Described as a "stately classical church in sandstone ashlar… with a plain and well-designed west tower".

Behind the pedimented portico, on four Tuscan columns, the nave rises to a broader pediment and behind this rises the beautiful west tower.

From 1764-8, the medieval chapel of St Ann was rebuilt to serve the rapidly increasing population of the Sandhill suburbs, by the river, of Newcastle. Described as a "preaching box, but a fine one", and designed by Newton, "in his usual, conventional but elegant, classical style".

The church has no separate sanctuary or aisles but it does have the distinction of a pedimented, Tuscan portico below a pedimented west gable carrying a tower with urns and a steeple.

Church of St Ann   (City Road)

Designed by William Newton and built between 1764 and 1768.

In 1820 a decision was made to demolish the Chapel of the Bridge of Tyne situated at the north end of the Tyne Bridge, Sandhill (- in 1770 the west end had already been demolished and in 1782 it had been further reduced in size).

At their own expense the Corporation of Newcastle decided to erect a new chapel at Barras Bridge on Magdalene Meadow, which belonged to St Mary Magdalene Hospital.

The Act of Parliament for the erection of the new chapel was given the Royal Assent on the 21st of June, 1827.

In July 1827, plans by the Newcastle architect, John Dobson, were approved by the Corporation to erect a new chapel. This would cost some £4,500 and would seat twelve hundred people.

Designed by Dobson and built between 1827 and 1830 it was consecrated on October 19th, 1830. It was described by an Edinburgh architect to John Clayton, the Town Clerk, as "one of the most chaste and elegant buildings of its size anywhere in the Kingdom".

Church of St Thomas the Martyr   (Barras Bridge)

Allsopp and Clark, in their book: "Historic Architecture of
Northumberland and Newcastle upon Tyne", pay the church a
mixed compliment – "The slenderness of the structure is
remarkable", they say: then add "the balcony was an unfortunate
addition".

Church of St Thomas the Martyr   (Barras Bridge)

The Church, left of centre, with the South Africa War Memorial on the right and the tall tower of the Civic Centre just to the left of the church.

Clavering House   (Clavering Place)

Before the arrival of the railway in 1849 Clavering Place was considered an extremely fashionable area of the town in which to live.

The house, of around 1748, is brick-built with two canted bays and a pedimented central doorcase. Above the doorway is a tall arched window with narrow, blind windows either side – rather in the style of a Venetian window.

Over an arched doorway can be seen a commemorative bust of the distinguished admiral.

Starting from the west end of St Nicholas' Cathedral and going down the Side – an extremely steep and narrow street, once the most picturesque in the town but now, alas, no historic buildings remain on this historic thoroughfare – you will pass the site of the house where Collingwood was born. The construction of Milburn House, by Alderman J D Milburn, in 1905, meant the destruction of both Bewick's workshop in St Nicholas' Churchyard and Cuthbert Collingwood's birthplace on the Side.

Collingwood was born here in 1748. He was educated at the Royal Grammar School then went to sea under Captain (later Admiral) Roddam. He fought as a lieutenant in the American War of Independence then was promoted Captain in the West Indies where he first met and became a lifelong friend of Horatio Nelson.

During his fifty years of naval service Collingwood spent fewer than six at home living, for a while, at his home in Morpeth. He was second-in-command at the Battle of Trafalgar (1805) when his ship, the Royal Sovereign, was so badly damaged in the fighting he was obliged to change vessels. By now a Vice-Admiral he took command of the fleet following the death of Nelson. He was given a peerage and died in 1810. He was buried in St Paul's Cathedral.

Built in 1864 in what was then the gardens of St John's Vicarage; the Royal coat-of-arms are mounted above the archway on the left. Two-and-a-half-storeys and five-bays the design of the south front (featured) is quite fascinating. The window surrounds on each level are quite different but it is the stonework on the ground floor which immediately catches the attention.

There is still a courtroom in the heart of the building though the original fittings are now gone.

Joseph Cowen was born in 1831 in Blaydon. He founded the Tyne Theatre and Opera House in 1867 and was the proprietor of the Newcastle Chronicle newspaper. He represented Newcastle as a Member of Parliament from 1873-86 and was considered a radical. Described as a social reformer he was a strong supporter of Irish Home Rule and freely espoused the cause of European revolutionaries. He particularly supported the struggle for Italian Independence. He also opposed Disraeli's Bill to make Queen Victoria Empress of India.

His monument, erected in 1906, stands just below Cross House, outside the Assembly Rooms. He died in 1900.

(Former)Dame Allan's School
(Northumberland Road and College Street)

Dame Eleanor Allan of Newcastle founded the Charity School of St
Nicholas when, by deed of gift dated the 20th of February, 1705, she
assigned a farm of some one hundred and thirty acres, at Wallsend,
for its support. Dame Allan died on the 21st of January, 1708, and
the school – for forty boys and twenty girls – was opened in 1709.

The school remained in Wallsend (the exact site isn't known) until
1786 when the Corporation provided a site at Manor Chare for new
premises, including living rooms for the Master and Mistress. The
school remained at Manor Chare until 1821 and then it moved again
– to occupy the Clergy Jubilee School in Carliol Square, which had
stood empty since it was built in 1820. In 1827 E Mackenzie tells
that there were now some four hundred scholars "learning to read
and write under the monitorial system".

Around 1860 the Clergy Jubilee School became a 'Trade School'
and shortly after the St Nicholas' Charity School was provided with
separate quarters in Rosemary Lane.

In 1877 the school was completely reorganised as Dame Allan's
Endowed Schools with a board of Governors, a grammar school
curriculum and permission to admit fee-paying pupils (- some fee-
paying scholars had previously been admitted to the Clergy Jubilee
School).

To meet these greater demands another new building was erected,
in 1882, on Northumberland Road where it remained until 1935
when, yet again, it moved – to Fenham.

(Former) Dame Allen's School
(Northumberland Road and College Street)

"A charming building, far more than the sum of its parts…"

(Former) Dame Allen's School
(Northumberland Road and College Street)

College House

- now a Security Office also handling Accommodation, Caretaking and Cleaning Services for the University of Northumbria.

Eldon Square   (Blackett Street)

Eldon Square was designed by Thomas Oliver, planned by John Dobson and built by Richard Grainger (1825-31).

In his book "New Pictures of Newcastle" (published in 1831), by Thomas Oliver, the author says of Eldon Square –

"Mr T Oliver (architect) was requested to prepare a design, plans of which together with a model of the same, were submitted for inspection at a meeting of the Common Council when the opinion of Mr John Dobson (architect) was taken, who afterwards furnished a plan containing several alterations… Eldon Square, with the exception of the centre building, is now complete: the three sides are of polished stone, to an elevation designed by Mr Dobson…". This extract from Oliver's 1831 publication seems to suggest that Dobson's role in the construction of the Square was no more than that of 'advisory architect' on the main plan and designer of the main facades – the main glory of Eldon Square.

The three great blocks of the Square, the east and west of twenty-seven bays and the north of thirty-nine, were each symmetrical, their angles accented with Doric pilasters. The first floor, with very tall windows, had cast iron balconies with Greek honeysuckle decor.

Eldon Square was unprecedented in Newcastle for its size, uniformity and building quality. Most of Newcastle's houses, at this time, were still built of brick: the houses in Eldon Square were faced with fine ashlar masonry – one of the earliest uses of stone for domestic houses in Newcastle.

On the centre block there was intended to be a six Ionic column portico – but this never materialised.

Archaelogia Aeliana (vol. XXIX) says that Eldon Square was Dobson's first known attempt at designs of town terraces, his previous practice having been entirely in the alteration and enlargement of country houses and the design of Presbyterian and Methodist chapels.

It is one of his best and we cannot now regret his poaching on what might have been (Thomas) Oliver's preserve.

Truly, these were fashionable terraces, described by one writer as 'the finest town houses built in the north'; and by another as 'the genteelist and best built part of town'.

Alas, only the east side of the Square remains: the remainder was completely destroyed in the 1960s by 'Philistines masquerading as developers and planners.'

The east side had twenty-seven bays: seventeen in the recessed centre and five in each projecting 'wing'.

The ashlar is of superb quality. The cast-iron balcony with its honeysuckle pattern links the pavilions at first floor level. Steps lead up to doors above basements protected by iron railings.

The wretched shopping centre that now bears its name was built between 1969 and 1975 and was the cause of the destruction of the north and west sides of a Square containing the most fashionable houses in Newcastle.

It is a late 17th century house with 18th and 20th century alterations. One of only two surviving seventeenth century brick buildings in Newcastle (the other is the Holy Jesus Hospital) with heavy moulded brick cornices on each floor and a parapet.

The house has small-paned, sliding sash windows, a main pedimented doorway – which is off-centre – and north and south projecting wings.

A 1723 map of Newcastle shows the house had both cupola and balustrade behind the pitched roof 'from which the Fenwick's would have had an excellent view of the river'.

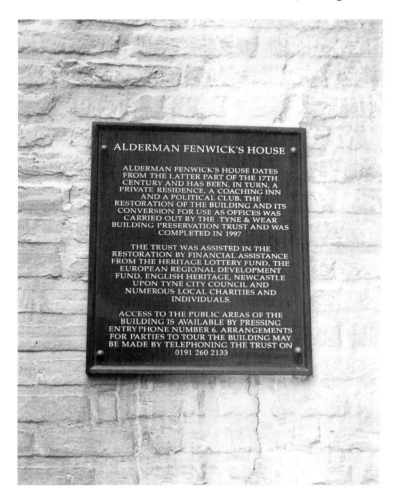

Described as "one of the grandest properties of its time" it is said to stand on the same site as the medieval Pilgrim's Inn.

In 1780 it became a coaching inn (the Queen's Head). From 1884 it was the Liberal Club, which it remained for some seventy years. It closed during the 1960s and in 1982 – after standing empty and neglected for twenty-five years – it was bought and eventually restored by Tyne & Wear Preservation Trust to something of its former glory.

The premises are now let as offices.

Protesters to the City Council's plan to demolish the only building
in the square which stood near the cottage where Bewick and his
family lived for thirty-one years (and which is long gone) and
which the engraver would still recognise, were he alive today, claim
it would be unthinkable… given the building's position facing the
newly named Thomas Bewick Square and the plaque.

The new Thomas Bewick plaque. The inscription reads:-

Thomas Bewick engraved the Chillingham Wild Bull on wood, in 1789. This large scale representation was made in 2003 to celebrate the 250th anniversary of the artist's birth.

The original block of the "Chillingham Bull" was unfortunately cracked through the thoughtlessness of an apprentice placing this on a window in the workshop, and owing to the large size of the piece of box wood used. The sunlight through the window was the cause of this. After repairs the line of the crack still showed on the engraving.

Forth House   (Thomas Bewick Square)

This part of the house is now the New Emperor (Chinese) Restaurant. There are plans (September 2003) to demolish Forth House, despite it being an 18th century building in a conservation area, to make way for a six-storey Chinese Church and twelve flats on the site, which faces grade I listed, St Mary's Cathedral.

Gateshead Millennium Bridge   (Gateshead on Tyne)

The fabulous Millennium Bridge (the now world famous 'Blinking Eye') is indisputably and entirely the property of Gateshead and, quite properly, the pride and joy of that Authority.

My impudent audacity in seeking to include it in a book on the "City Sights" of Newcastle does nothing to negate that fact. But I am sure (well, reasonably sure) that, the good citizens of Newcastle would raise no objection to any book on Gateshead including pictures of either the Tyne Bridge or the Swing Bridge even though, technically at least, both of these remarkable constructions are normally considered the property of Newcastle. It is a fact that Newcastle Corporation stipulated that no bridge support should be built on its Quayside (which some may have thought a little peevish) but since the north end of the bridge allows access to all Novocastrians as easily as it does their neighbours across the river perhaps I may be excused my effrontery. Besides, Gateshead Council have very graciously given permission for me to include my photographs of the bridge and I would hope the good people of that town would show equal amiability.

I include the bridge simply as, and no more than, one of the *sights* of Newcastle and I consider it a privilege to do so.

A design competition for the bridge was announced in August, 1996, and from a hundred and fifty initial 'expressions of interest' this figure was eventually reduced to six engineering and architectural design teams who then began work on their design concepts. These 'finalists' were given certain criteria within which to plan their design and the approval and co-operation of a number of other essential agencies was then sought as a matter of course. The six designs 'of varying ingenuity, grace and practicality' were duly considered by the judging panel and by other interested parties and the winner (the clear favourite) was announced in February, 1997.

The work on constructing the bridge was expected to be completed before the end of the year 2000 but, unfortunately, due not least to a delay in Government approval (which was only received in May, 1999), this proved to be an impossible target.

There were to be further delays of one kind or another before the bridge finally opened on the 28th of June, 2001 – though not to the public until September of that year.

The arch and deck of the bridge were fabricated at Watson Steel, in Bolton; the opening mechanism was manufactured in Sheffield and the assembly of the frame took place in Wallsend: the electrical and mechanical connections were added 'on site'.

In October 2002, the giant Dutch floating crane "Asian Hercules" arrived in the Tyne to transport the bridge from Wallsend upriver to its final position at Gateshead. Poor weather conditions meant a further delay as three consecutive days of ideal weather were considered necessary for this delicate operation. However, on the 20th of November the bridge was finally lifted.

The crane operator displayed tremendous skills and managed to lower the bridge to within one millimetre of its required position where it remained suspended until the tide fell and the final forty bolts were connected to their anchorages.

On June 29th the Guardian newspaper wrote: "The world's first tilting bridge (has) opened to shipping, not in some exotic transatlantic location but at the heart of a British region long famous for innovation: the north-east. The bridge links Newcastle and Gateshead, two towns which have for so long glowered at each other with unease and suspicion across the Tyne but are now... together, growing as bright and thriving as at any time in their history".

The Gateshead Millennium Bridge has received many justifiable compliments from all around the world: one, from nearer home, declares it – "A shining example of innovative architecture and engineering".

The bridge, which weighs more than 850 tonnes and cost almost twenty-two million pounds to build, was officially opened by Her Majesty Queen Elizabeth on the 7th of May, 2002.

With its approaches it spans the river a total of 413 feet (126 metres) and the main arch rises 164 feet (50 metres) above the water.

The motors for opening and closing the bridge are concealed in two concrete piers either side of the river; this operation can be completed in four minutes.

The structure comprises a pair of steel arches, one forming the deck and the other supporting it; the two being linked by thin suspension cables.

One enthusiastic critic described Gateshead's Millennium Bridge as a "contemporary design which complements the existing Tyne bridges in a way which is both refreshing and new".

I am confident both Robert Stephenson and William Armstrong would heartily approve.

The entrance off Grainger Street.

Newe House, or Anderson Place as it was later renamed by its
builder owner, was a mansion started in 1580, in the style of a
country seat laid out in a large, formal garden, right in the middle of
a crowded walled town.

By the 1830s and despite its apparent grandeur it had obviously
become an anachronism and if Richard Grainger's ambitious plans
for the development of the town centre were to be realised then it
had to go. He eventually secured its purchase for £50,000: the site
was to be the heart of his commercial and residential development;
a network of streets and a covered market designed by John
Dobson.

In 1834 the Corporation, encouraged by John Clayton the Town Clerk, did indeed accept Grainger's plans and on the 24th of October, 1835, at a cost of £36,290, within one year of the contract being signed, the Markets were officially opened. They were the most successful attempt at a traffic-free shopping precinct Newcastle had ever achieved, not only because owing to the low rents and overheads they could (and still do) sell goods cheaper than shops in the main streets.

The whole was contained within four streets of shops and houses "surpassing anything in street architecture hitherto witnessed in this neighbourhood". Many traders moved here from the Quayside, keen to take advantage of the new developments – at the same time accelerating the decline of the riverside.

Dobson's enormous covered market, protected by a massive glass roof, the largest in the Country, was of great architectural elegance. It covers several acres and the interior consists of five longitudinal avenues and four transverse ones, each twelve feet wide and present a succession of arched passages between the larger avenues.

The market is divided into two parts –the Vegetable Market and the Butchers' Market.

The open-plan Vegetable Market, with a complex roof structure, designed originally without the cast-iron pillars inserted, apparently at the request of the Corporation's architects (- the fine timbered roof has now, unfortunately, been covered by the Corporation) has an avenue which, according to Wilkes is 338 feet long; Faulkner & Greg 318 feet and Pevsner 313 feet: all agree the height to be forty feet. It contained 55 shops when it opened.

The Butchers' Market was housed in a network of four avenues each 338 feet long with pilastered arcades with classical detailing – 360 windows, fanlights and wood cornices. All told the Market contained 188 shops.

The writer, the late Jack Common, in his book "Kidder's Luck" (based on life on Tyneside at the beginning of the 20th century) gives a colourful description of the (by then, much changed) Butchers' Market – "A vast covered enclosure in which many sawdust-sprinkled aisles ran between the stalls, not only of butchers but book-sellers, drapers, ironmongers, cheap jewellers… glittering quicksands of proletarian penny-swallowing. The aisles echoed to the yells and yodels of salesmen, everyone of them selling cheaper than the man next door".

David Bean's colourful account of the Market's official opening tells us "The Corporation organised a grand public dinner inside and two thousand people turned up to admire 'the most magnificent markets in the world and the bazaar of shops within which struck the stranger with astonishment and wonder, beyond description".

There were two public dinners, in fact, both in the Vegetable Market – one at five shillings (including wine) the other at two shillings (including ale). The ladies were placed up in the gallery while fountains (copied from Rome's Borghese Palace) played below. Touts were selling tickets at three times their face value. "The effect", wrote one reporter, "was indescribably grand. The partial exclusion of daylight and the substitution of gas-lamps gave the magnificent scene a dioramic effect. The spacious roof, when the eye rested upon it for a few moments, seemed to rise into the air and the distance from one end of the hall to the other appeared amazing".

East side:

'The horizontal lines of windows between bands and cornices look especially crisp in such high quality ashlar.'

'The south corner of Market Street is an obtuse angle, turned by a gentle curve with a giant Ionic order on the upper floors.'

When Bainbridge's (now Kookai) was opened in 1869 Newcastle had the world's first Department Store.

The Guildhall   (Sandhill)

The original Town Hall, or Exchange, was built on the Sandhill, at the beginning of the 16th century. Adjoining the Exchange was the Town Court or Guildhall.

Thrice yearly meetings were held there by many of the town's incorporated companies: it was also the venue for the Mayor's Court, the Sheriff's Court, the Quarter Sessions and the Borough Courts, as well as other important, civic occasions.

This old Town Hall was demolished in 1655, probably as a result of the fire in 1639 which destroyed (among other things) the Town Clerk's office. In 1655, the Town Council ordered a new Town Court to be built. Robert Trollope, a mason from York, won the contract and a new 'Town Hall' was built, between 1655-58, at a cost of £10,000.

The Town Hall, or Guildhall, suffered serious damage in the hunger riots of 1740 and, again, in the fire of August, 1791.

As a result of these incidents the Common Council decided to reconstruct and "modernise" the entire north front of Trollope's seventeenth century structure (- other parts were altered later by other architects).

The old 17th century main entrance, with its twin-stairway, steeple and double-arched balcony were all taken down and replaced by a conventional, classical facade (designed by David Stephenson and William Newton, in 1794-6), set much further back and built in the same severe style as Newton's Assembly Rooms, on Fenkle Street.

They removed the stair-tower and rebuilt the entrance-stair using "an unfluted, giant, Ionic order", with a pediment.

To harmonise the north face of the main building with the new entrance (west of the stair) the existing, large 'Gothic' window had to be removed and the mullioned windows (another feature of Trollope's building) were all replaced by sash-windows.

They also encased the internal, ground-floor pillars, in sandstone, and generally smoothed out all the rustication to make a "more refined and fashionable building".

They also made a hipped roof out of Trollope's pitched one and added a small hipped roof to the stair forebuilding.

When Stephenson and Newton's alterations were completed the entire north frontage (on the Sandhill side) was left looking substantially, as it is today.

"Internally", writes H L Honeyman, "much remains of the gorgeous, if somewhat vulgar, piece of architecture, which Robert Trollope created… but, externally, it has been refaced in the more refined manner of the reign of George III."

The east end of the Guildhall is largely a neo-Grecian remodelling of Trollope's medieval-style, mid-17th century building, by John Dobson, in 1823-5.

The classical south-front (facing the river), of 1809, is the splendid work of John and William Stokoe.

William Newton and David Stephenson redesigned the north face in 1794-6.

The Guildhall of Robert Trollope bears little resemblance to the Guildhall of today; the north face of the present building was extensively remodelled and repaired in 1794-6.

The Corporation asked William Newton and David Stephenson to prepare a joint design, although the contract was drawn up solely with Stephenson. The design of the central part is very similar to Newton's Assembly Rooms: it is of five bays with the three centre bays separated by Ionic columns under a pediment. A plain, five-bay section extends to the west. Their work on the south front apparently only involved re-cutting Trollope's original stonework – and, in any case, it was completely refaced, in 1809, by John and William Stokoe.

A plain, five-bay section extends to the west.

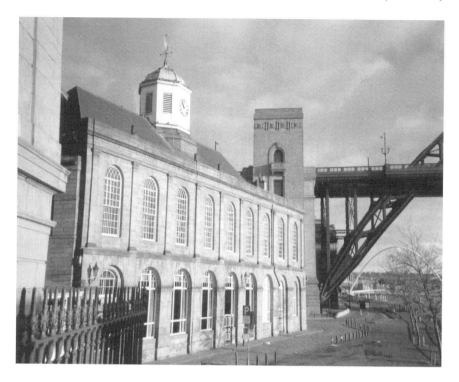

The south front, facing the river, with the Tyne Road Bridge and the new Millennium, 'Blinking Eye' Bridge in the background.

The first floor has nine, full-length, arch windows separated by Tuscan pilasters.

Newton and Stephenson were involved in re-cutting Trollope's original stonework but, in 1809, the south front was completely refaced by John and William Stokoe.

Richard Grainger, the son of a Quayside porter, started in business as a builder with his brother George, a bricklayer, as his partner. Shortly afterwards George died and Richard carried on alone. His first important contract was a commission to build a group of houses in Higham Place, for Alderman Batson, a prominent Newcastle Methodist. On its east side only three terraced houses remain of the row that was built for William Batson in 1819-20.

The brick-built houses have stone dressings and sash windows: the arched door-cases have pilasters either side and open pediments.

Pevsner described the short terrace as "a welcome oasis among the late 20th century hotels and offices".

Holy Jesus Hospital   (City Road)

The hospital is built on the site of the 13th century Augustinian Priory which, after the Dissolution, was retained by Henry VIII for the use of his Council of the North when it was not sitting in York.

It was founded and endowed by the Corporation of Newcastle in 1681 'to support poor impotent people, (39) freemen and their widows or their sons and daughters that had never been married'.

Holy Jesus is a brick-built almshouse, one of only two complete 17th century brick buildings to survive in Newcastle the other being Alderman Fenwick's house at Pilgrim Street – though the Keelmen's Hospital, on City Road, only just fails to qualify for this description, having been built in 1701. Around the first quarter of the 18th century the inmates received £4.00 per person per annum; by 1739 this had risen to six pounds together with a ton of coal at Christmas. In 1890 it is recorded that each occupant was paid thirteen pounds and three shillings (£13.15) and received four tons of coal per annum.

When the hospital was declared 'unfit' and closed in 1937 its resident thirty two sisters and eight brothers were transferred to the new Holy Jesus Hospital in Spital Tongues. The hospital on City Road then remained empty for a number of years and its condition inevitably deteriorated.

Money from the John George Joicey Bequest enabled a comprehensive restoration programme to be undertaken and in 1971 the Holy Jesus Hospital re-opened as the John George Joicey Museum.

Three storeys high with a Dutch gable at the end; all along the front
is an arcade consisting of thirty brick arches set on square pillars.
Above the doorway is a Latin inscription stating that the hospital
was built by the citizens of Newcastle, in 1682.

Just outside the hospital entrance stands a rather beautiful fountain.

The tower standing at the east end of the Hospital (properly called the Manors Tower but often called the Austin Friars' Tower, since the Hospital stands on the site of the old Augustinian Friary) is probably late 16th century.

In the south wall of the tower can still be seen a pointed, arched window – minus, alas, its tracery.

The Soup Kitchen (1880),

In the 18th and 19th centuries the land to the north of the hospital was occupied by the Poor House, a House of Correction (the Bridewell) and a Charity School – all of which have since disappeared – but in 1880 the Police Station adjoining the hospital to the west was replaced with a Soup Kitchen.

The International Centre for Life   (Times Square)

The entrance from Neville Street

The Centre for Life is a £54 million complex on a ten acre site (the size of a football pitch). It includes three distinct elements all exploring genetic knowledge – the greatest scientific discovery of all time.

The Heart of the Centre is an inter-active visitor attraction featuring six exciting zones – including a Gene Dome and Health Quest, a huge exhibition area. There is a Genetic Institute, housing the north-east's world class human genetic research and Bio-Science Centre.

The International Centre for Life   (Times Square)

The Life Science Centre.

The Lifelab (Education Resource Centre).

The Life Conference and Banqueting Hall.

The Bio-Science Centre (behind the Market Keeper's Office).

"An early, Italian Palazzo-style finance house", designed by
Benjamin Green and built c.1845 for the Newcastle Joint Stock
Bank.

With five bays and three-and-a-half storeys the plain, rusticated
ground floor has modern windows; those on the first floor have
keyed surrounds. The tall, sash windows on the second floor are all
pedimented and like those on the floor above have architrave
surrounds. The first floor is surmounted with a substantial stone
balcony from which lofty Ionic columns and panelled pilasters rise
up two storeys to a heavily modillioned cornice beneath a hipped
roof.

In 1697 the keelmen set up a charitable fund with which to build their own hospital. By 1701 they had raised sufficient capital to enable them to build the hospital, at a cost of some £20,000.

The Bishop of Ely is said to have remarked at the time that he had seen and heard of many hospitals, the works of rich men, but this was the first he ever saw or heard of, which had been built by the poor.

However, the keelmen were not allowed to administer the affairs of the hospital themselves despite the fact they had had both funded and built it. The social and political climate existing at the beginning of the 18th century made it impossible for a working class body of men like the keelmen to run their own affairs without surveillance and supervision (interference, even) by their 'betters'. This, not unnaturally, caused feelings of some bitterness on the part of the keelmen.

Trustees appointed to manage the hospital were members of the Company of Hostmen (coal owners) and the first Governor was Matthew White. For some years after its foundation there was friction between the keelmen and the hostmen over who should exercise control of the hospital's affairs. In 1710 a hundred men signed a petition 'complaining that the money collected for the hospital was partly detained and partly wasted and misapplied'. In 1723 the hostmen went so far as to pass a resolution that the charity should be run 'solely under their management'.

In 1730 the keelmen formed a benefit society and in 1788 an Act of Parliament was passed 'for the better regulation of the society', establishing a permanent fund for the welfare and support of the Tyne Keelmen who, through sickness, misfortune or old age, were unable to support themselves or their families.

It was inevitable that the importance of the keelmen should decline as more modern methods of loading the colliers on the river were adopted. The keels became redundant and finally disappeared.

The hospital is a fine, square, brick building, two storeys high and standing on a terrace looking out over the river and an area of the city where the keelmen once lived in crowded chares until the decline of their trade in the nineteenth century.

The building, which had been much repaired and restored and is now a student's hostel, stands now as a lasting memorial to a trade and body of men once an important feature of life on the river Tyne but whose place, nevertheless, is secure in the annals of Newcastle's long and colourful history.

An inscription over the doorway reads:

'The Keelmen's Hospital, built at their own charge Anno Dom. 1701.'
Above this inscription is a sundial and over this is a clock turret capped by a wind-vane in the form of a ship – perhaps intended to represent a keel or coal lighter.

The inscription on the stone tablet reads as follows:

In the year 1786
The interest of £100 at 5 per cent forever
To be annually distributed
On the Twenty third Day of December
Among the Ten Oldest Keelmen
Resident in this HOSPITAL
Was left by
John Simpson Esq. of Bradley
Alderman of this Town and
Forty Years Governor of the Hoastman's Co.

The bottom half of this inscription reads:

The grateful Objects of his remembrance
Have caused this Stone to be erected
That Posterity may know
The Donor's Worth
And
Be fumulated to follow
An example so benevolent

The east front of the hospital showing the splendid 18th century brickwork.

The building, which has been much repaired and restored and is now a students' hostel, stands now as a lasting memorial to a trade and body of men once an important feature of life on the river Tyne but whose place, nevertheless, is secure in the annals of Newcastle's long and colourful history.

The Gallery was the gift of Alexander Laing who gave it to his adopted city in gratitude and to commemorate a successful business career spanning fifty years.

It was opened by Viscount Ridley, in 1904.

Opposite the east side of Higham Place is 'the remarkable entrance and strong corner tower'.

The corner where Higham Place meets New Bridge Street has a
tower with rusticated ground floor. Below the octagonal lantern,
topped by a dome with a stone ball on top, and one hundred and ten
feet above ground level, is a frieze of carved figures symbolising
the Arts.

The Gallery was built between 1903-4 as an addition to the old Central Library, of 1884, which, like so much else, was demolished in 1968-9 to make way for John Dobson Street.

Leazes Terrace   (Newcastle upon Tyne)

Described as – "what is perhaps England's most splendid 19th century terraced development outside John Nash's contemporary scheme of Metropolitan Improvement in London, from Carlton Terrace to Regent's Park". The east side of this 'long hollow block' is 556 feet long with no fewer than eighty-six bays (an even grander scale than Nash's), projecting as it does into Castle Leazes "in a grandiose gesture of the picturesque imagination, injecting the purity of its classicism into the trees and meadows of the landscape".

'The architecture is finely and extravagantly detailed, the angles and centres of each facade are decorated with Corinthian pilasters and beautifully moulded frieze and cornice. The windows are simple and elegantly proportioned with a prominent piano mobile marked with a continuous highly decorative cast iron balcony. The stonework is finely worked in a very attractive honey-coloured stone.'

Designed by Thomas Oliver and built by Richard Grainger (1829-34) in the Palladian style 'these highly ornamented, pleasant and healthy ranges' are really quite uncluttered in their basic simplicity.

After a long period of neglect the terraces have been wonderfully restored by the University and the beautiful honey-coloured stone is as impressive now as it must have been when Grainger first used it.

The west front (featured) is overshadowed, intimidated even, by part of the new football stadium. Pevsner summarises the situation perfectly when he remarks: the concrete stand is "an interesting structure but a brutal neighbour".

The twenty-one bay, three-storeyed south front with fifteen bay centre block and projecting wings each of three bays.

Though far better known for his superb engraved maps of the city (apart from his involvement with John Dobson in the designs for Eldon Square little else of his work is of special merit) Thomas Oliver excelled himself in his design of the "magnificent 'square turned inside out'".

Lloyds Bank   (102 Grey Street)
Newe House (Anderson Place)

Newe House, or Anderson Place as it later became known, was Newcastle's most spectacular house. "The most stately and magnificent in the whole kingdom, within a walled town", was how one writer described it. Originally the land belonged to the Church but became the property of Robert Anderson, described as 'one of the wealthiest men in the town', in 1580. On the site of Greyfriars Monastery (- the Greyfriars or Franciscans, had arrived in Newcastle in 1274) and on the adjoining land of the Nunnery of St Bartholomew he built his Newe House, in the style of a country seat laid out in a formal garden – the site covered some twelve or thirteen acres – right in the middle of a crowded, walled town. The estate was purchased by Sir William Blackett, Member of Parliament for Newcastle and later owner of Wallington Hall, in 1675.

When his successor, Sir Walter Blackett, died in 1777 Newe House was sold to a rich Newcastle builder, George Anderson, in 1782.

When George Anderson died his son, Major George Anderson, inherited the estate and renamed his mansion Anderson Place.

For centuries this great estate had occupied virtually the whole northern part of the town frustrating any expansion at all along Newgate Street and Pilgrim Street: it had been an unwelcome impediment to the sensible planning and improvement of the town. Anderson Place was a 19th century anachronism, an obstruction that could not be tolerated any longer.

In the mid-1820s there had been discussions between Major Anderson and the Corporation about the possible sale of the house and grounds but these had come to nought as, at the time, the Corporation had other pressing, financial commitments.

Major Anderson died in 1831. Richard Grainger was still negotiating the purchase of the estate with Anderson's executors when he presented his proposed development plan to the Council on May 22nd, 1834.

In July of that year he took possession of the estate (at a cost of £50,000) and the Newe House was immediately demolished – with some help from a crowd of spectators gathered at the Nun's Field, who wrecked the inside of the mansion.

Grainger, with John Dobson's assistance, had proposed to build on the site a network of elegant commercial and residential developments, including a large covered market – the largest covered market in the Country. The Market (Grainger Market) was completed and opened to the public only fifteen months later: the remainder of his plan quickly followed – Upper Dean Street (later Grey Street); Grainger Street; Clayton Street; Nelson Street; Nun Street; Market Street; Hood Street and Shakespeare Street were all constructed relatively quickly. Indeed, people could only marvel at the speed and magnificence of Richard Grainger's achievements.

Anderson Place (the Newe House) stood on or near the site of the present Lloyds Bank on Grey Street: a bronze plaque on the south side of the building (on Market Street) records the site.

A bronze plaque around the corner, in Market Street, records the fact that this was the site of Anderson Place.

Built as houses and a bank on the site of the old Anderson Place, around 1839, in 1842 it was considered "the most highly ornamental building" in Newcastle.

Over a period of more than a century and a half it belonged to the Northumberland and Durham District Banking Company and Lambtons and Company Bank: it is now the property of Lloyds Bank who, in 1987, rebuilt the entire interior.

It is without doubt a singularly attractive building entirely unspoilt and in its original condition with neither unnecessary alterations nor inappropriate or unsightly additions to affect is appearance.

The ground floor on the west (Grey Street) front has four arched windows either side of the central doorway. The grandly impressive first floor consists of nine bays, all pedimented, and arranged in three groups of three, the central three slightly recessed behind the tall Corinthian columns.
Corinthian pilasters separate the other windows at this level.
Cornices separate the ground and first floors.

The second floor consists of nine small, nine-paned sash windows. Below the third floor attic another cornice, separating the second and third floors runs around all three sides of the building.

Built around 1839 on the site of the former Anderson Place it was, again, described in 1841 as "one of the most chaste and neatly decorated buildings in the town".

Remarkably, the architect is unknown.

A Memorial to the Royal Tank Regiment   (Newcastle upon Tyne)

Near the main door at the west end of St Thomas' Church and gazing out over the Haymarket stands a memorial to the men of the Royal Tank Regiment. Designed by J Reid and erected c.1920 the curved benches and plinths, on the top of which stands a bronze statue of St George, are made of Portland stone and granite.

Memorial to the Northumberland Fusiliers   (Newcastle upon Tyne)

In the grounds of St Thomas the Martyr and just to the north of the church stands a memorial to the men of the Northumberland Fusiliers.

The sculpture, by Sir W Gascombe John of c.1932, shows bronze marching soldiers their families clinging pitifully to their menfolk, against a block of grey Shap granite surrounded by an angel (Gabriel?) blowing a horn.

The buildings that make up the north side of Nelson Street are unusual in that they have been individually designed.

Right to left:

The Music Hall of 1838: next to it a warehouse of c.1899 (built on the site of a Methodist Chapel of 1837); then the Dispensary (later the Fruit Market or Exchange) of 1839; and finally the Cordwainers' Company Meeting Hall (the Cordwainers were one of the important medieval Guilds in Newcastle), again, of 1838.

The Café Royal – once the 'New Market Hotel'.

Charles Dickens, during one of his successful reading tours when his fame was at its peak and his books were selling in millions, appeared at the Music Hall for three nights during December 1861.

Tickets for admission were four shillings (almost a week's wages for some people) yet he was later able to write to his Newcastle friend, John Forster, that despite heavy expenses he had made more than one hundred guineas profit from his appearances. He also expressed his genuine admiration for the sensitivity and enthusiasm of his Tyneside audience who were, he said, among the best anywhere in the Country.

The Cordwainers' Hall of 1838.

The stone above the six-bay, central, first floor window reads –
Cordwainers' Hall. Wardens, Thomas Gilroy and John Walker,
MDCCCXXXVIII

The Cordwainers were one of the twelve senior medieval Guilds,
known as the 'Twelve Mysteries'. They represented the
shoemakers and were founded in 1556.

By the time the Hall was built they were the largest Guild, with 95
members, but they had become "mainly a ceremonial and property-
owning social organisation".

The Northumberland Baths, City Pool and City Hall
(Northumberland Road)

The south front is nicely symmetrical. Red brick with ashlar; the
'wings' (ie the Baths and the Hall) have matching, colonnaded
entrances with five square windows above. The projecting centre of
the building (the Pool) has five bays; the three central bays project
even further and are capped with a pediment with a circular window
in the centre.

The building was designed by C Nicholas and J E Dixon Spain and
built in 1928: the design has been described by one critic as "dull
neo-Georgian".

The Northumberland Baths, City Pool and City Hall
(Northumberland Road)

The ground floor of the City Pool consists of three tall arches
flanked by a tall window on either side with steps leading up to the
recessed entrance doors.

The Northumberland Baths, City Pool and City Hall
(Northumberland Road)

The City Hall (venue for musical concerts of all kinds), at the east
end of the block, is identical to the Baths at the west end.

About halfway down the street from the Haymarket, on the west
side, stands a shop built originally for Boots and Co. (the chemist),
around 1900. The top two storeys are unusually attractive because
of their window layout and stonework generally. Apart from these
features there are also four arched niches, two on each storey,
containing small statues of local heroes (top left and travelling
clockwise-): Thomas Bewick, Harry Hotspur, Richard Thornton
and Sir John Marley.

Thomas Bewick

He was born in Cherryburn House, Mickley, in the old parish of
Ovingham, in August 1753. The eldest of eight children he had two
brothers and five sisters. Their father was a farmer and landsale
colliery owner – a small colliery where the coal was sold directly
from the pithead and the customers usually collected it themselves.

Thomas attended school in Mickley though he was not a
particularly good student. He was bored by his lessons and had an
intense dislike of the schoolmaster whom he considered a bully. He
was regularly punished for playing truant. His parents transferred
him to the school in Ovingham but little changed. He still preferred
to roam the fields and lanes and riverbank and spent much of his
time drawing with chalks and pencil and pen and ink.

During a visit to Bywell in the Summer of 1767 William and Ralph
Beilby met a friend, Mrs Simons, who was not only the late vicar's
widow but also happened to be the godmother of Thomas Bewick.
She regaled the brothers with such a flattering description of
Thomas's artistic talents that they felt obliged to visit Cherryburn.
As a result of the visit on the first of October that year the young
artist left Cherryburn to begin an apprenticeship at the Beilby's
workshop in Newcastle.

Most of their work was done for gold and silversmiths but Thomas
soon became adept at engraving on wood and his master (Ralph
Beilby) grew steadily impressed by the lad's willingness to learn
and the quality of his work: so much so that he submitted some of
Bewick's work to the Society for the Encouragement of the Arts, in
London. Thomas won a prize of seven guineas – and this at a time
when, as an apprentice, he was earning only four shillings and
sixpence a week:

Bewick completed his apprenticeship in 1774 and quit the
workshop in St Nicholas' Churchyard to work from his home in
Mickley.

His fame as an exceptional wood engraver was already established among the fraternity of printers, publishers and booksellers in and around Newcastle and so for the next eighteen months he was kept busily employed. Then, in June 1776, he decided to go on a walking tour. He began in Cumberland, where he visited his mother's relatives. He then moved on to Edinburgh, calling at both Selkirk and Dalkeith, before continuing west up to Glasgow. Returning via Stirlingshire and Linlithgow he made his way to the port of Leith where he endeavoured to board a vessel bound for the Tyne. He reached South Shields on the 12th of August and arrived shortly after in Newcastle. He had been on his travels for some seven weeks. Two months later, however, he set off again – on a three week voyage by sea to London. Here, too, he discovered his good reputation had preceded him and so during his time in the capital he was never short of either work or the companionship of close friends. But, after nine months, his dislike of London and, more particularly, too many of its inhabitants drove him back to Tyneside where he was offered regular employment by one of Newcastle's leading publishers. It was at that time (1777) he went into a successful partnership with Ralph Beilby, back at the workshop in St Nicholas' Churchyard.

In 1785 Bewick's mother, father and eldest sister all died and so his hitherto frequent visits to Cherryburn all but ceased.

His marriage to Isabella Elliott, the daughter of an Ovingham farmer, took place the following year when he was by then living in the Forth – one of the more fashionable areas of the town (a site now occupied by part of the Central Railway Station). Thomas and Isabella produced one son (Robert) and three daughters (Elizabeth, Jane and Isabella).

In 1795 Thomas' brother, John, whom he had taken as his apprentice on his return from London, died and was buried with other members of the family in Ovingham.

In 1821 the entire Bewick family moved from the Forth to a large house in West Street, Gateshead, which remained the family home until 1883.

Sadly, only five years after the move to Gateshead his beloved wife Isabella died.

Though still interested in his business Bewick was now an old man and the general running of his affairs was now in the capable hands of his son Robert, himself a good engraver. Thomas rarely visited the premises in Newcastle content to work from his home in West Street where he died in 1828 at the age of 75.

This "truly original genius" produced a wealth of brilliant work during his lifetime. Perhaps his best known works are and will always remain – his "General History of Quadrupeda" (1790); his "History of British Birds" (1797 & 1800); his "Fables of Aesop" (1818) and his "A Memoir of Thomas Bewick" – written by himself – which was only published, in 1862, thirty-four years after this death.

Harry Hotspur

It was during the reign of Richard II, after that monarch had invaded Scotland and burned Edinburgh, that, taking advantage of England's subsequent weak and disorganised state brought about by inept government, the Scottish nobles – led by Earl Douglas – with an army of some four thousand men crossed the Border into England.

The plan was simply to lay waste to Northumberland, plunder and destroy as much of it as possible then, if at all possible, seize the town of Newcastle. The Earl of Northumberland, Lord Percy, despatched his two sons – Sir Henry (known as 'Harry Hotspur') and Sir Ralph – to confront the enemy.

Henry, one of the finest soldiers of his day and recognised as a brilliant strategist, stationed his forces in Newcastle, determined that the Scots should not take the town.

During one of the many skirmishes outside the town walls Hotspur, having challenged Douglas to single combat, was unhorsed and lost both his spear and his pennon (a long, swallow-tailed, triangular flag) attached to it. Douglas, taunting Sir Henry, waved the pennon aloft crying, "I will carry this token of his prowess with me to Scotland and place it on the tower of my castle at Dalkeith, that it may be seen afar".

"By God, Earl of Douglas", replied Henry, "you shall not even bear it out of Northumberland; be assured you shall never have this pennon to brag of". Next day the Scots moved north to Ponteland where they burned the village and fired the castle. Then they proceeded to Otterburn some thirty miles from Newcastle. Hotspur would have pursued them immediately had his chiefs not urged caution warning that the Scottish army might be many times greater than their own small force.

"Better to lose a pennon than a battle which would leave the country defenceless," they argued.

The battle of Otterburn (better known as the Battle of Chevy Chase) was not one of the great battles of history, more a typical border fray.

Hotspur eventually followed the Scots from Newcastle with a force of 600 spearmen and 8000 infantry. After a long march he reached Otterburn at night and though his men were understandably exhausted he decided to attack the enemy by moonlight.

In short, the battle – which was fought on the 19th of August, 1388 – was, from the English point of view, a shambles and a disaster.

Earl Douglas was killed and Ralph Percy captured: the English army was routed. They lost almost three thousand dead; another thousand were taken prisoner. The Scots had less than one hundred men killed.

In 1402 the Scots again invaded Northumberland with a larger force numbering almost ten thousand.

Again they pillaged and plundered and again they reached the gates of Newcastle. On their return to Scotland they camped near Wooler but found any further progress blocked by the forces of the Earl of Northumberland and his son Sir Henry Percy ('Harry Hotspur').

There followed, on the 14th of September, the Battle of Homildon (or Humbleton) Hill, which, on this occasion, was a disaster for the Scots. Many prisoners were taken and hundreds were drowned trying to cross the Tweed.

The Percys quarrelled with the King over the prisoners: the Earl wanted to ransom them (as was the custom). King Henry wanted to keep them as hostages in future negotiations with the Scots. Northumberland and his son made a secret agreement with their old enemy, Douglas, and the Welsh, to depose Henry. But while the Anglo-Scottish army were moving to join their other allies in the Welsh border Henry's army intercepted them in Shrewsbury and in the ensuing battle, Harry Hotspur, the famed Northumbrian knight, was killed – less than a year after his brilliant victory at Homildon.

Sir Henry Percy, known throughout centuries of history as 'Harry Hotspur', the eldest son of the Earl of Northumberland, is best remembered for two reasons (apart from his prowess as a knight): the part he played in the Battles of Otterburn and Homildon Hill and the fact that he has been immortalised by Shakespeare in the bard's play 'Henry V'.

Richard Thornton

Newcastle's own 'Dick Whittington' was a poor boy from Northumberland – possibly from the village of Netherwitton, or Witton as it was then; a few miles west of Morpeth – who came to Newcastle to make his fortune and ended up not only "the richest merchant that was ever living in Newcastle" but also the town's first Mayor. In fact he was elected Mayor on no fewer than eight occasions, a record which has never been surpassed.

Not much is known of his early life. In 1394 his name appeared in local records as part owner of a ship, "The Good Year".

What is known is that he seemed to succeed in his every venture and enterprise: he truly had the 'Midas touch'.

When Henry IV became King, Thornton was chosen by his fellow burgesses to represent them in Parliament. He leased lead mines in Weardale, from the Bishop of Durham; he was a ship-owner; he dealt in corn and imported wine – it was even suggested he was not above a little piracy, though this may well have been a scurrilous story circulated by jealous business rivals. Investing in property he acquired Wingates, Witton, Stanton (all west of Morpeth); Horsley, Stannington, Benton, Killingworth and Plessey, "besides houses and tenements in London and Newcastle".

"He enjoyed", it is said, "a prosperity not seen again on Tyneside until the Industrial Revolution".

Richard Thornton built the Guildhall, on the Sandhill, for the use of the Merchant Venturers and the town's various guilds. He also built a hospital on the Sandhill, known as the Maison Dieu (or Maison de Dieu) or Thornton's Hospital.

He married Agnes Waunton (or Wauton) and they had several children. Agnes died in 1411. Richard succeeded his wife another thirty years and died, in either 1439 or 1440, in his house in Broad Chare.

Both Richard and his wife were buried in All Saints Church, where a handsome tomb was erected, only the brass of which survives. His vast fortune was inherited by the only one of his children to survive his father – Roger Junior.

Sir John Marley

John Marley was the son of William Marley, a 16th century Newcastle merchant, who died in December 1609 and was interred in St Nicholas Church.

An inscription on the family tombstone states that Sir John was "83 years and three days" old when he died: he was buried on the 24th of October, 1673, so it may be deduced that he was born on the 19th or 20th of October, 1590. Regarded as something of a local hero Sir John nevertheless appears to have been a not all-together 'wholesome' personality and there occur numerous references to the less savoury side to this character.

He was engaged in the coal trade and in 1634-5 was appointed Sheriff of Newcastle. In 1636 we learn he was fined by the Hostman's Company (the coal owners) "for fitting other men's coals". Yet despite this the following year he was appointed Chief Magistrate and the Hostman elected him their Governor. Shortly after this he was appointed Mayor of Newcastle and is described as 'a man of energy and resource and a strong supporter of Church and Crown'. Indeed, in July 1639, as a reward for his 'loyal services' the King rewarded him with his knighthood.

In these troubled times between Crown and Parliament Marley kept an active watch over his sovereign's interests in Newcastle and was foremost in everything that tended to help the Royal cause – troop movements, munitions, plans for the town's defences, and so on. He was regarded by the King's advisers as a trusted friend – not an opinion shared by the Earl of Northumberland, who believed him to be an ignoble charlatan. When Lord Conway arrived in the town to assume the command of the King's forces he would have taken up quarters in Marley's house. The Earl warned him that Marley was intent on selling corn of a very inferior quality to the army. On investigating the Earl's claims Conway found it to be true. The Earl said of Marley – "If I thought it possible for a man who has lived twenty years a knave to prove afterwards an honest man I should entertain a more charitable opinion of Sir John Marley".

Not long afterwards the Scots took possession of Newcastle and Marley was said to have fled the scene. In May 1642 he was summoned to appear before Parliament to answer an indictment brought against him by his Puritan fellow townsmen. The House considered the charge proven and in September he was ordered to appear again – 'but of the summons he took no notice'.

A month later, for reasons not explained, the King insisted he should be reappointed Newcastle's Mayor: he was re-elected accordingly, again being appointed Governor of the Hostmen. When his year of office expired he was again elected and he was occupying this post in January 1664 when the Scots crossed the Border and invaded Northumberland.

The account of this siege of Newcastle is well documented and has been related many times: a comprehensive description is not, therefore, needed here.

On February 3rd, 1644, the invading army appeared before the town and summoned it to surrender. A force of only fifteen hundred men were able to hold out against an army of thirty thousand for the next ten weeks.

To be fair to Marley it was said, 'he himself was at the heart and soul of the defence' and worked indefatigably to organise the townsfolk and their resistance. Many times the town was called upon to surrender 'and as many times did the brave mayor refuse' 'though the demands of the enemy were seconded by the supplications of the suffering people'.

The Scottish Commander, the Earl of Leven, now issued his famous threat to destroy the lantern tower at the top of St Nicholas Church if the town refused to surrender. Marley judiciously placed Scottish prisoners at the top of the tower and defied Leven to butcher his own men: the tower was not fired upon. However, on the 20th of October, the town – except the Castle Keep, to which Marley and his officers had retired – was overrun. After four days Marley and the others offered to surrender if they could be guaranteed a safe passage to the King. The offer was refused and they had no option but to surrender unconditionally. As they emerged from the Keep they were violently attacked by an angry mob who, 'having discovered how he had deluded them', blamed him for their sufferings during the siege.

Marley was committed to the Tower of London but somehow managed to escape abroad where he was later joined by his wife and family. His estates were sequestered and later sold.

At the time he was described as "a proud and insolent Mayor" and "a notorious and infamous delinquent". He remained in exile for twelve years then, with the Restoration of the Monarchy his own former rights and privileges were also restored.

On April 10th, 1661, he was elected one of the town's Members of Parliament and later that same year was, for the fifth time, elected Mayor of Newcastle. He remained a Member of Parliament until his death in October, 1673.

The north side.

The south side.

Police Headquarters (Newcastle Central Area Command)
(Market Street East)

A very plain, unprepossessing construction compared to the
Magistrate's Court and the Fire Station on Pilgrim Street. Five
Storeys and sixteen bays. This is the third Police Station on the site
since 1840.

A colourful and detailed contemporary account of the Arcade was published in the Newcastle Daily Journal, on the 19th of May, 1832 – it reads:

This magnificent building, now the scaffolding in front is removed, and the various works approach to a completion, has excited the liveliest emotions of pleasure in the minds of the inhabitants of Newcastle, and the admiration of every stranger.

From its situation, the magnitude, the splendour of the front, the beauty of the interior – with the long row of conical windows in the roof throwing a rich stream of light upon the chequered marble pavement beneath – and the excellence of its arrangement throughout, the Royal Arcade cannot fail to become a prominent ornament to the town and an object of attraction to every intelligent visitor. Were we to omit all record of so spirited an undertaking we should neglect a portion of our duty, and we have therefore been at some pains to collect the following particulars, which we have pleasure in laying before our readers:

The front adjoining Pilgrim Street and facing Mosley Street is of elegant polished stone, 94 feet wide and 75 feet high. The architecture of the basement storey is of the Doric Order, with an enriched entablature surmounted with six fluted, Corinthian columns. On the attic is a beautifully turned balustrade, also of stone, in front of which, in the centre of the building, is to be placed a group of five figures, 'Britannica' being the most prominent. The rooms on the north side of the entrance will, we learn, be occupied as the banking home of Messrs. Backhouse & Co; and those on the south side as the Savings Bank: over which will be three large public rooms.

The interior of the Arcade is 250 feet long, 20 feet wide, 35 feet high having conical, ornamental skylights raised upon an arched, groined ceiling richly furnished with pure Grecian ornament.

On each side of the Arcade are eight large and elegant shops, the first and second storeys having been arranged with every convenience for offices. At the east end of the Arcade are a suite and splendid apartments comprising a News Room, an Auction Mart, a room for public purposes 72 feet by 32 feet with ante-rooms adjoining. Above, there is to be a conservatory, with Medical Vapour and warm and cold baths adjoining. Underneath the whole of this splendid line of buildings are large arched vaults with offices, the entrance to which are by Manor Chare.

Some idea may be formed of the great skill, assiduity, and judgement by which the various operators have been directed by Mr Grainger, when we state that, although all the apartments, offices, shops and public rooms are expected to be fully occupied in the course of a few weeks, it is not yet twelve months since the first stone was laid. The munificent spirit by which so great a public ornament has been directed, and so much public accommodation provided, will not go unappreciated.

If only this glowing and enthusiastic testimonial had been corroborated by unfolding events – but, alas, it was not to be.

The rather sad history of the Arcade is well documented. Other fulsome descriptions of it can be found in Faulkner and Greg's excellent book, published to celebrate Dobson's bi-centenary, in 1987; "John Dobson, Newcastle Architect, 1787-1865"; "Newcastle upon Tyne: Northern Heritage"; and Lyall Wilkes' and Gordon Dodds' "Tyneside Classical".

From designs by John Dobson work had begun on the site of the present-day Swan House, at the bottom of Pilgrim Street, in June 1831 and, remarkably, was completed just short of a year later, in May of 1832.

This was a shopping arcade the like of which Newcastle had not seen before even though it was not uncommon in the fashionable capitals of London and Paris.

It was, without doubt, a major contribution to the town's public architecture and was closely based, so we are told, on the highly successful and prestigious Lowther Arcade, in London – yet, it was deemed to be (particularly in the manner of its lighting) superior to the London arcade and thus was recognised as being the finest in the Country.

It cost close in the region of £45,000 to build it. It housed not only shops but offices and other amenities – banks, auction rooms, a Post Office and a steam and vapour bath. The interior was floored with chequered stone and black marble and it was lit by eight conical skylights set in domes high up in the roof. There were eight shops on either side of the mall.

Unfortunately, however, despite its impressive appearance and many attractions Richard Grainger, the builder of the Arcade, had neglected to give proper thought and consideration to its siting – an oversight which was to have disastrous consequences.

In fact, the Arcade experienced commercial difficulties, as a result of its unpopular situation, right from the beginning, and it was therefore never the commercial success it was confidently expected to be.

The Daily Journal's correspondent boldly forecast that 'all the apartments, offices and shops … are expected to be fully occupied in the course of a few weeks …'; yet by 1841 (nine years later) some of these same shops had still not been let. The Post Office vacated its premises in the 1860s and gradually, one after another, the offices emptied until the end of the century they were almost exclusively occupied by "furniture brokers and second-hand dealers".

Demolition of the entire Arcade was seriously proposed as early as the 1880s. Having been left to gradually decay for several decades (- it was described by N Tarn, in the Northern Architect of March, 1963, as "an embarrassing white elephant") it was finally demolished in 1963.

During demolition each stone was carefully numbered and stored with the intention of rebuilding the Arcade elsewhere – but it never happened. All that now remains (though it, too, has been abandoned at the time of writing) is a replica of the interior of John Dobson's original Royal Arcade. Situated as it is beneath Swan House, ironically and arguably the ugliest building in the whole of Newcastle, this now deserted 'fake' actually cost more to construct that the elegant original.

The fact that the Royal Arcade was a commercial failure, practically from the outset, was due entirely to the unusually bad judgement shown by Richard Grainger – the man who, probably more than any other, was responsible for bringing so many other wonderful buildings to the town and city of Newcastle.

Quite simply, he built the Arcade in the 'wrong' part of the town, or, as The Penny Magazine so aptly and succinctly put it "… he (Grainger) failed in this one instance to take sufficient notice of both topography and trend".

'The front (of the Arcade) to Pilgrim Street dominated the 18th century houses of the street rising to a height of 75 feet with giant Corinthian columns above a severe Doric ground floor. A heavily ornamented cornice, a balustraded attic storey and a coat-of-arms, by Dunbar, lay above. A similar block at the far end of the Arcade, at a lower level, faced Manor Chare.'

(Faulkner and Greg)

"One of John Dobson's most dignified compositions" – Faulkner and Greg

It was decided to commemorate the Diamond Jubilee of Her Majesty Queen Victoria, in 1897, by raising sufficient funds for the erection of a new infirmary. To the sum of £100,000 which was raised initially, a further sum of £100,000 was given by John Hall Esq and one other sum of £100,000 was subscribed by Mr and Mrs W A Watson-Armstrong, bringing the grand total to no less than £300,000.

This new infirmary (the Royal Victoria) was a major step by Newcastle Corporation to help raise the city's health standards – which, at that time, left a great deal to be desired. The Corporation and Freemen provided a ten acre site at Castle Leazes and work duly began in 1900. The Hospital, designed by Newcombe and Adams, was completed in 1906 and was officially opened on the 11th of July, of that same year.

Since 1906 there has been a never-ending catalogue of extensions, improvements and developments of every description needed simply to keep pace with the hospital's ever widening expansion of its activities.

For example, shortly after the opening, in 1907 the Electrical Department was 'up and running'. In September 1918 a Massage School was founded. The Nurses' Home, which had opened in the hospital grounds in July 1905 was enlarged in 1931 by the addition of the Runciman Wing. Also in 1931 the erection of a new block to provide accommodation for twenty-eight medical staff was completed and, that same year, the opening of the Leazes Hospital with three pavilions, an operating theatre and eighty-six beds.

In 1933 two new wards were built, an Orthopaedic Block with forty-eight beds was opened, an out-patients' department, an operating theatre and a fully equipped massage school were all added to the hospital buildings.

The development of this fine teaching hospital (for that, too, is one of its functions) since 1906 has been and is still ongoing.

The Department of Pathology has been extended; the Department of Radiology and Bacteriology expanded and the Department of Anaesthetics and of Psychological Medicine long since established. And so it continues.

A notice outside the hospital on Queen Victoria Road, seen in August 2003, proudly proclaims that between April 2002 and the Spring of 2003 an investment of some three and a half million pounds allowed major refurbishment works to existing buildings, including the Dermatological and Geriatric Wards, Children's Out-patients and Dialysis, Cleft Lip and Palate.

Progress in the fields of medicine and surgery is often breathtaking verging on the miraculous and for almost a century the Royal Victoria Infirmary has been in the vanguard of these developments. The hospital inspires both trust and affection in the hearts and minds of those many thousands of her patients who, every year, are simply grateful that it is and continues to be so.

The Administration Block is the most impressive building in the hospital complex. Built of red brick and ashlar the roof covered with grey-green Barrowdale tiles, the style is Baroque.

The imposing west front (featured) has a porte cochere in the three-bay centre with hipped roofed pavilions at either end of the seventeen bays. Pediments above the ends and centre are supported by pilasters.

The roof has attic windows, four tall brick chimneys on the west side and a central lantern.

The statue of Queen Victoria, standing on a terrace in the centre of the garden and directly in front of the porte cochere, was the gift of Sir Riley Lord. Designed by George Frampton it was erected in 1906.

The buildings on the Sandhill (right to left) are as follows:

Number 32 on the extreme right, is the Red House (a Bar); next to it is Bob Trollope's Restaurant and Bar; the red building between the two 'Tudor' buildings is the Quilted Camel (a Bar): on its left, with the attic window, is number 44, 'Offshore' (another Bar).

The next two buildings are both the property of English Heritage:

the first is Bessie Surtees House (once Milbanke House), the other is the four-and-a-half storey building next door; on its left is Carmichael's (a Bar/Café); next to it is the six-bayed Waterside Hotel, which in the photograph appears to be white but is actually bright yellow: the ground floor of the hotel is 'Breeze' (a Bar/Café). The last building in the block (only the roof of which can been seen), is a five-bay, three-storey building called 'Jimmy'z Bar' – then we reach the Castle Stairs.

Built in 1830 to designs by architect John Dobson.

An ashlar-fronted terrace in Tudor style. The majority of ground floor frontages have given way to incongruous and rather gaudy 'shop fronts'. Fortunately, however, a few of the originals still exist: *Midland Bank, for example, has preserved the original doorway with its flight of stone steps flanked by iron railings.

(* now HSBC)

On an island between Westgate Road and Neville Street the bronze statue of the great inventor stands, resting his left hand on a roll of plans, on a pedestal around the base of which are the figures of a miner with Stephenson's 'Geordie lamp'; an engineer holding a little locomotive; a navvy grasping a length of rail and a smith with hammer and anvil. The monument was erected in 1862, at a cost of £5,000, and the sculptor was John Graham Lough, who also designed the statue of Admiral Collingwood to be seen gazing out to sea at Tynemouth.

The Sutherland Building
(Northumberland Road and College Street)

Named after Sir Arthur Munro Sutherland; designed by Dunn, Hansom & Dunn, the foundation stone was laid by the sixth Duke of Northumberland on November 3rd, 1887.

Dark red brick and red terracotta, with ashlar dressings; the style is Gothic. The entrance tower is rather like a gatehouse. The windows have mullions and transoms and there are gargoyles below the battlemented parapets of the central and corner towers.

The Sutherland Building
(Northumberland Road and College Street)

Designed as the University of Durham Medical School (just below the two chimneys in the centre of the gable just around the corner in College Street, are inscribed the letters D.U.C.M. – Durham University College of Medicine). The building now belongs to Northumbria University and houses the School of Law and the Departments of Student Services and Learning Resources.

The present building, said to be "distinctly more Victorian than Georgian in the way it dominates the street", is Newcastle's second Theatre Royal. The first was a Georgian brick building situated midway along Mosley Street. Built by David Stephenson and opened on January 21st, 1788, it had a relatively short life and was demolished in 1836 to make way for Richard Grainger's Grey Street. The present theatre, by Benjamin Green (with some assistance from his father, John), was started in July, 1836, and opened on February 20th, 1837, with a performance of Shakespeare's "Merchant of Venice" – remarkably, the theatre was completed in less than eight months, though the magnificent portico was not finished until December of that year. The portico has six great Corinthian columns, with two outer pairs rising from huge, moulded plinths. The columns support a triangular pediment containing the Royal Arms, carved by C J Tate of Newcastle, who was paid eighty-five pounds for his craftsmanship and another five pounds for the stone he used.

Corinthian pilasters frame the outer bays of the theatre's frontage, which project rather like pavilions surmounted by balustrades. The whole front is beautifully symmetrical in appearance.

The theatre's design is described as being at one with the rest of the architecture in Grey Street.

On November 24th, 1899, tragedy struck when the wonderful period interior was destroyed by a fire which gutted the theatre. Restored in 1901 the interior was once again remodelled, in 1987, at a cost of £6,333,000.

On its grand reopening on January 11th, 1988, the theatre staged "A Man for All Seasons".

This theatre is one of the largest and most beautiful out of London; as the portico projects completely over the foot pavement and is formed wholly of enriched stonework, it constitutes one of the greatest ornaments of Grey Street.

(The Northumberland Directory of 1854).

The magnificent Tyne Bridge, which is synonymous with
Newcastle and the pride of all Tyneside, was opened on October
10th, 1928, by His Majesty King George V. Designed by Mott, Hoy
& Anderson and built between 1925-8 by Dormon, Long & Co of
Middlesbrough it contains some four thousand tons of steel and is
described as "a striking engineering achievement".

The broad roadway, eighty-four feet above the river, is suspended
from a gigantic yet graceful steel arch, rising in the centre to a
height of one hundred and ninety-three feet above the high water
mark. The 'ends' are deeply sunk, almost seventy feet below the
water level, in concrete, below massive twin piers at either end of
the bridge – which is some 1,254 feet long.

There was a considerable destruction of buildings on both sides of the river to make way for what has been called "the model for the bigger Sydney Harbour Bridge (in Australia)", though it is not an exact prototype as there are notable structural differences and even at 4000 tons the 'Tyneside colossus' could easily be lost inside the girders of its Australian counterpart.

Not so long ago it was possible to travel from the Quayside to the bridge in a lift in one of the towers – for the princely sum of three old pence.

One of the four great stone piers or towers, two of which are at either end of the bridge. This one stands on the east side of the Newcastle end of the bridge.

It is said that the Tyne Bridge carries more traffic than the Humber, Severn and Forth Road Bridges combined.

The postern gate in this tower was used to "sally forth" and attack besiegers; hence the name the Sallyforth Gate.

In 1714 the Ships Carpenters (or Shipwrights) Company of Newcastle needed a new Meeting Hall and began to raise money to build one. In 1716, having raised sufficient funds, they built "a grand and stately square tower, adorned at the top corners with four fair turrets, built in the form of a lanthorn".

Pevsner describes it as a "curious structure, built on top of the Sallyport to create the Sallyport Tower". He adds that the Shipwrights built their "superb, bold Hall" above the minor gateway, "in such confident style that comparisons have been drawn with the work of Vanburgh".

The principle features of the Hall – the set of three, round-headed windows; the large areas of rustication and the pyramidal corner towers - strongly suggest the influence of Vanburgh, it must be admitted, but as yet the architect remains unidentified.

On the east side of the tower (left of picture), steps lead up to the Hall door, above which is a rusticated cornice. Above the cornice is a carved relief of a ship's hull – proclaiming the company's trade: this may explain why, locally the building was often called the Carpenters' Tower.

Tomlinson describes it as "a picturesque object".

The north front.

These late 18th century buildings, built originally as houses but with 19th century shop-fronts added, are a valuable reminder of a period when Westgate Road was an extremely fashionable, residential area.

The red building (number 60), just in the picture on the left, has been described by one writer as "an attractive piece of late 19th century fancy"; and, again, as "a jolly, vaguely French style, office building which neatly punctuates the south side of Westgate Road".

Second from right (numbers 77-79) is the Star Inn: it has had a somewhat chequered architectural history. Originally dating around 1860 it was restructured internally both in 1937 and again in the '50s when a pub front was added – this has been subsequently altered with, perhaps, greater success. The brickwork of the three 'houses' in between was painted in rich colours after the fashion of the 1960s and is both tasteful and arresting.

Bibliography

I feel it is unnecessary to list every book referred to for useful information. The following are those most frequently consulted and I am deeply grateful to the authors and their publishers.

The Buildings of England: Northumberland; Pevsner et al (Penguin, 1992)

The Buildings of Grainger Town...; David Lovie (North East Environmental Education Forum, 1997)

Lost Houses of Newcastle and Northumberland; Thomas Faulkner & Phoebe Lowery (Jill Raines, 1996)

Newcastle upon Tyne: Its Growth and Achievement; S Middlebrook (Newcastle Journal, 1950)

Northumbrian Heritage; Nancy Ridley (Robert Hale, 1969)

The Tyneside Classical Tradition (Designed and Published by Tyne & Wear County Council Museums, 1980)

Newcastle 900: A Portrait of Newcastle upon Tyne; David Bean (Newcastle upon Tyne City Council, 1980)

Newcastle upon Tyne; Peter Winter, David Milne, Jonathan Brown & Alan Rushworth (Northern Heritage Consultancy, 1989)

Men of Mark Twixt Tyne and Tweed; Richard Welford (Walker Scott Ltd, 1895)

Newcastle Town; R J Charlton (Walter Scott, 1885)

Famous Northern Battles; written and published by Frank Graham (1970)

Comprehensive Guide to Northumberland; W W Tomlinson (W H Robinson)

Crossing the Tyne; Frank Maders & Richard Potts (Tyne Publishing)